Tamanna Sharma, born in the serene embrace of Dehradun, began her poetic journey at a tender age of twelve. Despite being surrounded by the breathtaking beauty of the Himalayas, her verses often delve into the realms of introspection and darkness. *Whispers from a Grave* unveils a selection of poems from Tamanna's school days, offering a glimpse into her innermost thoughts and emotions, as conveyed through the ink of her pen.

WHISPERS FROM A GRAVE

TAMANNA SHARMA

AMARYLLIS

AMARYLLIS
An imprint of Manjul Publishing House Pvt. Ltd.
• C-16, Sector 3, Noida, Uttar Pradesh 201 301, India
Website: www.manjulindia.com
Registered Office:
• 2nd Floor, Usha Preet Complex, 42 Malviya Nagar, Bhopal 462 003 – India
Distribution Centres
Ahmedabad, Bengaluru, Chennai, Hyderabad,
Kochi, Kolkata, Mumbai, Noida, Pune

Whispers from a Grave by Tamanna Sharma

This edition first published in India in 2024
Third impression 2025

ISBN 978-93-5543-825-6

Cover Design: Neelima P Aryan

Printed and bound in India by Repro India Limited

Dedicated to the souls who
carried their verses to their graves.

Introduction

The idea of doing this book took shape in my mind, way before I even started writing poems. I believe poems are a reflection of the heart, and as a person who feels deeply, my heart has been writing poems for a long time now. However, it was only when I turned twelve that I started letting my poems manifest on to paper. One paper turned into many, and when I had enough to call it a collection, the idea of this book was finalized. It was only a co-incidence that I finished school the same month this collection was completed. One can call this a collection of my poems from my school days. But, the grave that whispers to me was never my school; it has always been I, myself. It was also my wish that the cover of this book be kept dark to represent the darkness a grave holds within. I have not put in the effort to arrange the poems in a manner that represents any sequence or rhyming, because much like any other human being, my life has never been a straight line – it has always been a chaotic symphony. To arrange these poems in any order would be an insult to my own life. Every page is meant to represent a different day, and with it, a different emotion.

And the one subject that becomes the center of my poems, again and again, is death. I would, however, like to clarify that death is not my muse, because my poems are what make me come alive.

Hence, I write only for one thing, and one thing alone... Life.

Today,
the wretched night
appears
eternal.
Dressed in a long white veil,
that haunts me to death.
For it is
when she lifts it up
and
breathes life
into the ghosts of my futility
that I had buried
somewhere in the walls of my room.
They rise up again
only to remind me
I am worth nothing.
In silence
they speak to me,
in words that make my ears bleed,
my heart twinge,
and my eyes shed tears of ashes
which have been birthed by
the raging fire burning inside me.
They grab my morbid throat and choke down
the sword of verses I had gathered to slit theirs.
I do not scream for help,
I do not die either,
outside.

Sometimes,
I forget to return the things I've borrowed from people.

Borrowed happiness,
to linger around town as clouds of love in the air.

Borrowed love,
to adorn their withered souls.

Borrowed smiles,
to alleviate the deepest scars that they carry.

Borrowed melody,
for their hearts to dance their lives away.

Borrowed books,
for them to read the eyes of their beloved.

Yet,
borrowed pain,
chokes down my throat.

I have heard folklores and tales
of a witch
who ran away into the woods
and devoured her own self.
And now
there is a prophecy around the town
that the witch shall be born again.
But
what if she never died?
What if she still lives in me
devouring me, instead.
I am a folklore
a newly birthed prophecy,
I AM HER.
Like her
I wish to vanish into the woods
of death.
I yearn for the ground beneath me
to split open
and engulf my flesh and bones.
I can feel my skin moulting.
Slowly.
And yielding to her a new disguise.
As days pass by, I melt into oblivion.
The crooked-toothed witch laughs at me,
she has swallowed my heart,
taken away my flesh
and stabbed my mind.

Will she take away my soul, too?
I
AM
HER.
Perhaps,
she, too, may
become me.

To all the people
who call me a friend:
My dear ones,
I could never be a good friend to you,
a someone who I always aspired to be.
My misery turned me into a monster who ate alive
all of its affection.
Despite that I tried..., I tried to be there for you,
even when I was lost myself.
I am still searching for my mere existence,
I wanted to bring light to your world
consumed by evils of dark,
even though I was deprived of light in my own.
I wanted to quench the thirst of your parched land,
even when my own barren land howled for rain.
I never wanted to see tears in your eyes,
even though mine, bottled up inside... only to burst in
solitude.
I gave my all to it,
yet,
I could not make the twain meet.
And now I wish to dig a grave
and
bury myself there.
My dears,
you must pity such a friend.

What do you want to be when you grow up?

Kind.
Kind to myself.

I have inflicted a million stabs and bruises upon
her,
I have destroyed and killed myself for nothing.
I speak to her
with venomous branches entwined in my lungs,
which poisons my inner voice.
Her mistakes trigger volcanic eruptions in my
mind,
whispering that she is worthless.
I anticipate her to be flawless,
her imperfections bring forth my inner demons,
urging them to emerge and bury her soul.
So yes,
when I grow up,
I want to be kind to myself.
I want myself to lover her imperfections,
to understand
that no every day has a colorful sunset,
even dark clouds merit love.
And
within love's embrace, bottled up emotions find release,
transforming shadows into
a rainbow.

I belong to simple everyday moments,
while the world is out there engaged in chasing big dreams.
I belong to the twilight sky,
which fills color in my mundane thoughts.
I belong to the old wooden house on the crest,
which has harbored generations and still stands tall.
I belong to the carnations someone brought for their beloved,
plucked from the garden which has grown inside their heart.
I belong the stationary tree on the roadside,
which has a myriad tales to tell.
I belong to the giggles of little children playing hide and seek,
a laughter which is the most real thing in the world.
And I belong to the eyes of the aged man sitting in his balcony,
wise eyes, that have seen all seasons of life.
I belong to the dark abyss in the forest,
where I find the light inside me.
I belong to my bedroom window,
which is a gateway to the exploration of my dreams.
I belong to the setting sun,
which bids a farewell meltingly.
I belong to the smile of my mother,
when I tell her she still looks young and beautiful.

I belong to the wiggle of a dog,
when I pet it gently.
I belong to these little moments,
which, in fact, are not so little.

The leaves
of the autumn of love
have fallen into a winter of
an unwavering hope
to glimpse sunlight again amidst
eternal darkness.
This cold air brushes
through my morbid, freezing cheeks,
and I pause and ponder
if it is a gust of your
warmth, from miles away, yet, so close.
The dreamy silence in this street of our existence
yearns for the giggles of a children's park,
and the dying joy of this old soul
longs for the living strength of the youth.

But what is more tragic
than my fondness and craving for death
is that no matter
how many
fireflies I am adorned with,
the numerous stars that shine
bright
inside my eyes,
birthed by bleak black nights,
which I have buried
my numb face in,
and the sun
I have let burn
inside me
to illuminate
my cold skin,
they who indulge will never acknowledge my light.
For them,
I will always remain
a mere gust
of insignificance
which is
visible, yet invisible.

My school has raised
its boundaries
adjacent
to the river,
the very same river
which flows away
the boat that carries
the cargo of my memories here,
and brings it back with a mere glance at the pristine
waters.
I can no longer gaze
at the
crystal waves
shining
as sunbeams penetrate them,
flowing east.
With no worries of encountering
my hardcore nemesis,
I can no longer
look out of my classroom window
to watch
the dazzling blue flow.
And contemplate its exquisiteness
and let my heart
pour
down a poem
about it.

This feeling of being deprived
of beauty
that adds
meaning
to your day
pushes me into dejection.

I wonder if my friends feel the same?

Or have the raised boundaries raised
the longing
of their hearts
and yearning
in their eyes
to see
the serene landscape?

I am no less than a corpse alive.
In the day,
with my cold skin decaying leisurely.
Bones breaking down,
and turning into stone.
My heart pumping blood bitter and blue,
that turns my eyes grey,
my vision blurring against bliss.
My soul counts each breath of mine backwards,
the insides of me howl and howl like hungry wolves.
I am
turning
sick
of this wretched cosmos
dwelling inside me.
My old friend death, where are you?
I wish to see you again.
Let me be free
of this wretched world
inside,
and
lend me another.
Death slowly invades my mind,
and I behold the last few pieces of me
vanishing at the threshold
into the woods.

Moonlight emerges
from the dark
and touches my face.
I see again the lost parts of me
reviving and returning from where they once began,
my eyes pleasured by beholding this delightful world.
I feel again air of life within my lungs,
my blood is red, like a thousand crimson roses
blooming.
The moon brings back life into my lively dead
corpse,
once again.
And I see life –
Real Life...

When you'll be standing
before
the door
of death,
and on the other side Hades,
awaits to wrap you in his arms,
tell me my friend, would you remember your
marks?

In your balcony,
in the autumn
of your life,
days falling and fading so fast,
would you count the money you earned?

Young man,
I presume
you won't.
Years from now,
when you look back
to these days,
you will fondly recall the peals of laughter
and people's smiles beaming
each smiling,
each laughing,
yet, each decidedly different.

Do not only merely exist,
live.
Live these days
to the fullest,
my friend.
For memories are a ride into the past,
so make sure,
you make
good ones till the end.

Mother,
if words were venom,
you would have killed me a million times by now.
Your malicious words coming out of your sweet
mouth to grab my throat and choke me to death.
They are like the demons that haunt me each night.
I run. I run as fast as I can,
but they grab me and bury me in a dark grave.
And still,
the only name I yearn to for help
is yours.

Deep inside the chambers of my heart,
rage reigns
and swallows
each heartbeat,
a fiery rage that grief has yielded.

He... extinguishes that fire in me.

Sometimes,
I am
my own demon.
I cut
my veins
and entangle them to
restrict myself.
I let my blood
spread
across
the floor,
to walk on it
and let myself slip
into the dark dungeons
of my own mind.

He... draws me out of it and kills
this demon in me.

There are days
when a chaotic storm
of my thoughts
engulfs me
and turns me blind.

He... becomes my eyes
in that storm.
He... is the calm
in the storm.

The whirlpools
in the ghostly
sea of my tears
deluge me,
threatening to bury me within them.
My lungs gasp for air,
He... swims across
the storming sea and rescues me,
I bury myself in his arms.

He... breathes, and breathes me back to life,
once again.

Tell me, dear sky,
for how long have you been bottling up the clouds
of emotions
behind the curtain
of your dense pink canopy,
that you burst so recklessly today?
Tell me, dear sky,
for how long have you been told to
shut your mouth and suffer in silence,
that today the stiches tore apart
and you roared in agony?

What a wonder it is,
that you have not a clue
that someone,
somewhere,
from the core of their heart,
writes about you.

A secret admirer
or a long-lost friend?
and how you lie in the words of their poetry,
in each phrase, until the end.

In the notes and journals,
in the depth of the pages
with every drop of ink,
love buried since ages.

They don't express the affection,
instead, get it down on the paper with bliss
and you still have not a single clue about it,
oh, what a wonder it is!

If thee shall take my life, take it away
if thee shall cease my breath, cease it
if thee shall tear my flesh, tear it apart,
if thee shall cut my veins, go ahead
if thee shall plunge a knife into my heart, do it
if thee shall pluck out my eyes, gouge them.
But do not kill me by taking him away from me,
do not kill me by snatching away my soul.
For I must only live
with him by my side,
and I must only breathe
feeling his breath upon my skin,
and I must only smile,
with him holding my hand.
O my dear, do not kill me by taking him away from me.

When I am sitting
alone,
not in solitude
but in loneliness.
Consumed
by reading,
just to conceal
myself into a fictional world, where misery seems
bearable.
You approach me and remark that I look sad,
perhaps intoxicated
with some melancholic substance.
At that very moment, there is a sprint
of thoughts across my mind justifying my
desires and everything I wish to do.
I wish to slit my wrist and
let the bad blood burst out of it,
only to fetch it and drink it down my throat again
and set ablaze my heart.
I wish to let that fire, burning deep inside me
set every pore of my existence afire,
and burn it completely.
I wish to pierce my chest
and tear apart
my lungs
filled with air of agony
you breathe around me.

I wish
to jump off
a bridge
into the river of my own tears,
to drown
into its bottom, and hide there.
Too many things I wish for,
but worst of all
I wish to kill myself,
to entirely erase my existence.
Regretfully, my cowardice does not allow
a painful death.
So, I wish
someday
sleep comes and take me
gracefully away, and I never return again,
I lie there, in a deep and peaceful sleep.
Peacefully.
Forever.

Dawn knocks at the door of my grave,
and I see a sunbeam penetrate my skin
and bring back to life the soul of an artiste dead.
Inside me,
alive, once again.
I crawl back
to another day,
and deliver art again.
I breathe in pain,
and exhale art.
With a paintbrush plucked out of my nerves,
I paint the misery on the canvas
of my skin with the myriad colors of my blood.
The ink of my vein summons
the cold-blooded universe,
and turns it cordial
with its warmth.
And as footsteps of dusk approach,
I dig a grave while dancing on my feet
to bury myself there with an unheard melody.
From my grave, moonlight emerges
only to illuminate the world after my demise,
but you see,
my addiction to art never lets me die.
After my death
my art
makes me alive.

Perhaps another dawn
shall come again,
looking for me
tomorrow,
to lend me
another day
to bury myself
in art.

I went into the woods,
in search of you.
In search of you,
I lost myself, too.

The forest saw me,
an enemy without arms,
I had neither you nor myself,
though I never meant any harm.

I stood a wanderer,
deep inside the forest.
Roots
entangling my feet.
Branches
locking up my wrists.

DÉJÀ VU!

Perhaps, I have been here before,
entangled in your ignorance and deceit,
the branches let go of my hands,
the roots freed my feet.

Stuck there in the woods,
I befriend the trees and the dark,
the solitude and the serenity,
and nature's art.

I feel something
that I haven't felt in ages,
I feel alive and I feel the warmth of my soul,
as if I were a bird
freed
from a cage.

And I have been to the woods,
in search of you.
You were gone,
but I found myself, though.

I died before death
could find my door.
In a single lifetime, I have lived and died a million
deaths before.
Yet, no one noticed my corpse,
so alive it looked
and breathing as it was.
In a dark cave,
I would not have looked
out for a flicker of light,
if only I had known
it would be
the reason
for my demise.
All my un-alive life
I yearned for a home,
a home far
from the mortals,
far, somewhere all alone.
I found it in a graveyard
yet, they never buried me there,
and death still dangles around my throat,
killing me every day.

I am like a farmer,
thirstily awaiting the rain.
And you,
the dark clouds of monsoon,
but sadly, in a different sky again.

You will rain
but your raindrops
won't land
on my ground,
won't touch my skin,
they won't make the soil of my earth aromatic.
I'm forbidden to have you, as if I've committed a sin.

I do long for you,
but I never will kneel before you,
for I am strong enough
to hold myself
together
in my blues.

And the beat of my heart
will be louder than the sound of your empty
thunder.
The light in my eyes
will outshine,
the bolts of lightning in your otherwise dark sky.

You may call me heartless,
but you carry not the same pain
inside your chest as mine,
I wish I could read you my poetry
and you could comprehend it and whine.

Understand the depth
of each verse, each syllable,
and relate to
the anguish
in my veins,
this bleeding heart would find a companion to
share the pain.

I wish you could dive deep
into my heart,
and see
the broken pieces
buried deep inside,
and I could dive into yours,
to fix the fragments you have tended to hide.

I ask myself,
am I transparent enough
for them
to peek
into the hell
burning
inside me?
With the flames of diffidence
and insecurities
burning the insides of me.
Is the cosmos inside me, where self-hatred dwells
visible
in plain sight?
If it is, then I must find it a veil,
for its exposure enhances my insignificance.
But,
why do I expect them
to accept me
when I keep
running away
from my own self?
Why do I expect them
to love me when I engulf my own self
into a whirlpool
of self-hatred?
Why do I expect them to
consider me worthy
when I myself don't know my own worth?

Perhaps worthless I am,
but why do I expect them to
look for me, when from my own self I yearn to
disappear?
And why do I expect them
to let me live
in harmony when I myself long
for death
in serenity?
I do wonder,
if this twinge of hatred
for my existence
exists within them, too?
I presume,
I give my all
just to be invisible,
and as I let my emotions flow with ink,
I bottle up the tears
on the brink of shedding,
for I believe
I become
more transparent
with every tear I shed.
Perhaps, this transparency will pave a way
to a higher mutual hatred.

If I am to choose
between
the starry skies
or your eyes,
no doubt
I would
love to
see a sky
abound
with stars
of love and faith.

And if I am to choose
between
the virtues of heaven
or a slight glimpse
of you,
no doubt
I would
bury
my eyes
in the heavenly sight
for seconds.

And if
I am
to choose
between

a library of a thousand
books
or a momentary glance at your visage,
no doubt
I would
spend
the moment
deciphering
scrambled
words
on your skin.

And if
I am
to choose
between
a life
without you,
or a death
by your hands,
I would
love
to get a knife plunged in my chest by life itself.

Somedays, I wish
my sluggish friend death
could come and meet me,
or I could find
an easy ride to its house.
Or I could simply just say its name
and it could
come and clutch me
in its arms,
taking me to a place I seek.
A place where my breath
slowly loses its rhythm,
a place where my skin
becomes gradually cold
and I turn
numb.
A place where my lungs
cease gasping for air anymore,
and my eyes bid a fading farewell to light.
Perhaps today
is the day?
I know not.

When she was young,
her mother stayed by her side until she slept.
For she was afraid of
the monsters
underneath her bed.

Scared of the night,
she wanted the day to last long.
For in the gloom,
she had to pretend
to be strong.

But soon she wasn't
afraid
of darkness,
nights became her companion.
The toxicity of the world
transformed her heart
into a canyon.

Merry she looked in the daytime,
the nights saw her whine.
And the monsters she was once afraid of,
became
her partners
in crime.

And now she knew,
and felt real dread
of the Monsters
of the World,
not the ones that she once thought
were underneath her bed.

Full of thoughts,
abounding with fret.
My head is a prison,
I wish I could escape from it.

No, I don't have a nemesis out there,
but it's up here with me.
A residence of angels and devils,
and for help, I make a plea.

It's a cluster of chaos,
where heaven and hell lie,
A whirlpool of emotions,
the joy within slowly dies.

All the pain and anguish,
I let flow onto the pages
all the bruises and scars
I have been carrying since ages.

My wounds are deep
my heart is a void
a pain deep within
I tend to avoid.

My soul screams,
as does the silence
it bears the agony
like a lone island.

All the happiness,
and healing I desire
we say we are happy
no, my dears... we are all liars.

Mother,
tear my flesh
and bury my bones
in your skin.
Take me back into your womb,
to the realm of my existence.
It is high time that I merged into you,
perhaps we'll be more alike then.

This mayhem inside me
and the one I create
around me,
would succumb ultimately then.

Father,
am I even worth your sweat?
or am I a pure disgrace?
for what I have perceived,
I am all vain.

Did I ever make you proud?
no, I couldn't.
come, stab me
to death
if you will,
slit not my throat with your words,
for the scar that you paint with it,
reminds me of my futility.

I believed,
if not the world,
at least you would have faith
in this morbid soul.
But, I have been delusional all this while.
The gardeners
of this plant
stopped
watering
it a long time ago.
You have already killed my lively spirit,
now come,
come and burn away
all the flesh that
remains.

My grave is a
cradle of the poet dwelling inside me,
every drop of poison
I consume
is ink to her,
the blades
I cut myself with
is her pen.
Born of the depths of despair,
she gives life
to my dead notions.
every death
of mine
is a flicker of a
new existence
for her.
I burn silently
in the fire
of an excruciating agony,
and she engraves
my secrets
with the ink
of my own poison.
And throws
the paper
in the silent fire
where I burn.

I see
myself
burning
with my thoughts
that succumb to the fire,
raging with poems,
I'll never
read you,
with lines
I'd never
write again,
they all
die with her.

Inside a shattered heart
dwell the demons of
grief and agony,
my heart pierces itself
apart,
to banish
those demons
and the smell
of warm blood
turns it cold.
The raging flow
of the
roaring red river carries away
with it all
the anguish and rage.
Piece by piece
the desolate, dead heart
stiches itself together.
This time, it dares not to love again,
rather it craves more to be loved,
it craves to be held
tenderly,
in delicate hands
but fears
the stiches could tear apart again.

And if some day,
the sun stands up on the pedestal of pride,
boasting of its scintillating light, brightening up the
earth,
I would still tell him about your smile.

And of envy,
he would hide somewhere behind the clouds,
to see if in his absence the entire world trembles
beneath darkness's shroud.

But, oh, you poor sun,
you would die of envy each time,
to see how my world lights up
with his bewitching smile,
sans compare.

Father,
what do you do of a wretched child
who brings you nothing but misery,
do you throw him away into the woods,
or do you let the poison
slipping out of your tongue do its own magic?
For the seed of poison
grows not
into a rose,
but a deadly nightshade,
whose leaves tangle around my morbid nerves
slitting them in succession.
But you worry not,
for I will let not blood flow out
into the world,
rather,
I will paint the walls of my room red with it
and decorate it
with a hanging antique,
a living corpse.

Mother,
I wish you could see
the world through my eyes,
and live it in my skin.
Perhaps then you would choose
honey over poison
to embellish your words with.

If I cannot be a good human,
let alone a good child,
O mother, swallow me
into to your womb
and birth me again.
Perhaps, this time I will not return
as a wretched child.

I was in a different world last night,
darkness consuming the woods
and the fog blurring my sight.
From the woods emerged a voice
calling out my name.
And I was certain of its existence, I know from
whom it came.

The voice penetrated my soul,
and for a moment, it made me feel
light and complete.
And then I was sure,
the voice I was completely swallowed by,
was yours.
I went searching of you,
unfortunately bereft of any clues.
And then my eyes
flickered with a sudden glow of light.
And it wasn't sun, but your eyes so bright,
which took away all clouds of darkness
descending upon me.
But then, I realized it was all a dream.

So yes, you were in my dreams last night,
and intervened in a vicious fight.
A battle between my demons and I,
I was saved from myself,
I am obliged to thee.

The broken glass
of my window,
is a boat
which sails across
the sea of memories,
it takes me back
to the days when I played
cricket with my father
in the garden, and we broke
a window pane.
The sudden reminiscence
breeds
nostalgia and laughter in us.

The broken pieces of my mirror,
show different pieces of me,
each exhibits
a part of me
which got lost
somewhere on the runway of life
and I realize,
I am the protagonist
to a thousand tales...,
tales of despair,
tales of bravery,
tales of love,
tales of laughter,
and tales of what not.

The cracks
on the walls and ceilings
of my ancestral home,
whisper lores into my ear,
they tell me, how resolute they have been.
Surviving the harsh rains
how valiantly
they have been sheltering
the gentle snow,
and how patiently
they have been enduring
the scorching heat.

They tell me tales of the laughter and giggles
of children running around the house,
subdued plaintive crying of folks bidding farewell
to their loved ones,
they tell tales of the lives and deaths of generations seen.

The broken watch of mine,
gifted by my aunt,
now lies somewhere
in my cupboard,
portraying the reality of life...,
no matter how broken anything is,
time never waits.

It carries forward leaving behind the gift of beauty.
Broken things are the most beautiful,
for they encapsulate
countless untold, unheard stories.

I had hidden
behind
a veil of coldness,
and locked
the doors
of my compassion.
I had built
walls that were unsurmountable.
Love?
I stopped looking for it,
I had eradicated the word from the kingdom of my life.
Yet, one day, love showed up
on the threshold
of my barren heart land.
It knocked,
once,
twice,
thrice.
I kept the doors closed,
until I realized,
perhaps
this time,
it wasn't
agony disguised,
I unlatched the door amidst the four walls of my house,
inside which I had kept myself captive.
On the brink stands your home,
said my conscience to me.

The spring of hope,
blossomed back in this land,
of gloomy winters.
the flowers bloomed,
the birds sang again,
the sun felt warm, not harsh,
the air kissed my dead cheeks,
the butterflies played
with strands of my hair.
From my grave, I woke
from a nightmare
that had lasted quite long.

I like it
when it rains
but I love
the deafening sounds
of the rain,
gentle raindrops,
hitting hard the ground,
as if they are resentful,
like my mind resents me.
But
for some reason,
the roaring downpour
subdues
the loud voices
of my mind,
and breeds a momentary peace.

And when I lay on my death bed,
and death I shall await,
as I count my last heartbeats,
would you come to me, mate?

We'd reminisce about our days
and the memories we made.
Peaks and valleys of life,
what a beautiful trade.

And I would ask for your forgiveness,
from a heart left with but a few heartbeats.
For if I had ever hurt you in past,
in afterlife, I shall make amends if we ever meet.

In the last moments of life,
before I join the stars above,
tell me I mattered,
tell me I was loved.

Tell me I made you laugh,
tell me I made your day, sometimes.
Tell me you were happy in my company,
tell me I was your best partner in crime.

For this is all I shall take with me,
and this is all I shall leave behind
the good deeds and memories
and no regrets left in the mind.

And when my eyes close
never to open again,
and I am devoid of life
do not grieve, my friend.

Our heart forbids acceptance of death
but death is the truth and intense the pain,
but by grieving for the dead,
let not your life go in vain.

I wish you were
my sleep paralysis demon
visiting me in the dead of night, each day
filling my heart
with a sigh of relief
at your divine sight.
I believe
your presence
won't scare
me to death,
unlike
the daily visits
of the creeping demon
underneath my bed.
And then, I won't be afraid to sleep,
and in my sleep, I will not weep.
Perhaps the sudden constriction of breath will
make me
more alive
than I ever was,
and I won't gasp for air anymore.
My frozen body is forbidden movement
and when I scream
I can't be heard,
the restraint on my body
feels like a caged bird now emancipated...
the shadows twirling feel more like fairies
dancing in the dark,

and I don't cry for help, I sing like a lark.
The ache in my nerves
and heaviness
on my skin,
feels more like the gentle tenderness of your holy touch
and the warmth of your grin.
For once, I beg not for this nightmare to end,
and this time I wish not to wake up again.

We are as much dead
as the ones buried and earthed, yet,
the only difference is,
the echos of their souls will live,
while ours will have
died even before they were buried.

We are akin to those entombed in the soil,
we have been screaming to be let free of this
confining coffin.
And the only difference is,
they are alone,
and we are lonely.

How many times
have I found shelter
in a pen
than
in people.
Everywhere I turned for solace,
I was disowned
by their words.
The words
they never gave life to,
but echoed only through their eyes.
People,
they are beautiful,
still, at times
they make me sick to the core.

I exhibit my agony,
in form of my art.
and you call it beautiful,
this raging torment of
my aching heart.